The Middle School Rules of

THOMAS MORSTEAD

as told by

Sean Jensen

BroadStreet
KIDS

Alex,
I hope you enjoy this book
Love,
Grandma
8-26-2020

BroadStreet Kids
Savage, Minnesota, USA

BroadStreet Kids is an imprint of BroadStreet Publishing Group, LLC.
Broadstreetpublishing.com

The Middle School Rules of Thomas Morstead

© 2020 Thomas Morstead and Sean Jensen

978-1-4245-5900-8
978-1-4245-5901-5 (e-book)

Back cover photo by the New Orleans Saints. Used with permission.

Design by Chris Garborg | garborgdesign.com
Editorial services by Michelle Winger | literallyprecise.com

Printed in the United States of America.

20 21 22 23 24 25 26   7 6 5 4 3 2 1

TABLE OF CONTENTS

INTRODUCTION

Dear Reader,

I can vividly remember being in elementary and middle school and not feeling confident about how I looked, dressed, or acted. I endured verbal and physical bullying, and I witnessed even more examples of both, so I know how challenging that can be to deal with.

I learned very early on to follow my internal compass, regardless of what my peers said or how they treated me.

As you read through my childhood experiences, I hope they give you the confidence to stick to your own convictions.

Growing up, I always loved sports and saw myself as an athlete. But I wasn't physically capable of competing at a high level throughout my childhood.

I was a zero-star recruit in high school.

That ended up being a blessing in disguise because I had to focus on academics as my pathway to success.

Thankfully, I wasn't alone. You're going to read about all the incredible people who helped me through my difficulties, starting with my parents. These people fueled me throughout my childhood, providing big and small doses of encouragement that shaped my life.

I hope you enjoy my story.

WHO DAT!

Thomas and I first met in fifth grade when both of our families were invited on a ski trip. I remember his teeth stuck out, his voice was high-pitched, and he was, to be honest, kind of annoying.

Years later, during my sophomore year in college, my mom called me after attending the 21st birthday party for the son of the family that invited us on that skip trip. My mom saw this tall, handsome man and asked someone, "Who is that?"

"That's Thomas Morstead."

She went up to Thomas and introduced herself as my mother.

"Oh, I remember Lauren," Thomas told her. "She was my first crush."

That was all my mother needed to hear! She basically gave Thomas my resumé and said how amazing I was. She told him we should become Facebook friends and hang out.

When she told me, I was mortified.

"You did what?"

I love so much about my husband, but my favorite thing about Tom is that he knows who he is and he isn't afraid to be himself.

Tom isn't the greatest dancer and it's not something he likes to do. But I *love* dancing. Our first dance party in college was an 80s-themed dance. It took a while for our new dating jitters to get out of our systems, but eventually I dragged Tom onto the dance floor. He was unapologetically himself, terrible dance moves and all. Weirdly enough, the more he danced, the more I fell in love with him. His rhythm was so out of sync. He knew it and he danced confidently anyway. He did it for me, and he never got embarrassed about it. We danced and sang "Don't Stop Believing" at the top of our lungs.

Tom taught me to be unapologetically me, and he has loved me in my best and worst times. He showed me how to be confident in myself and in my worth. He has been such an inspiration to me, and I am excited for others to be inspired by his story as well.

People often ask why we are so committed to our nonprofit: What You Give Will Grow. Thomas and I have much to be thankful for, and we just don't see how we could not be passionate about blessing others.

To whom much is given, much is expected.

FOREWORD BY
John Morstead
FATHER OF THOMAS MORSTEAD

You always wonder what your kids will be like when they grow up.

As a boy, Thomas was a pretty good soccer player. But in those early years, I hadn't seen sheer determination or aggression from him.

Will he be timid? Or will he stand up for what he wants and push forward?

When he was 10 years old, Thomas was on the wing, and he was going for a 50-50 ball. I looked at his face, and I could see his will and fight to succeed. He won that ball, and I remember thinking, *He is going to be fine.*

From there, you could see how he went about his business—whether soccer, football, or his studies. He was willing to go the extra mile and forego unimportant things to achieve his goal. Sometimes when you're younger, it's hard to see the big picture, but Thomas has always been able to focus and put distractions aside. I don't know if stubborn is the right word, but he definitely gets that trait from his mother.

Something else that makes me proud of Thomas is how thoughtful he is. When the New Orleans Saints won Super Bowl XLIV in Miami, our family headed to the After Party. Thomas was anxiously looking for his mom. When he saw her, he didn't say, "Hey, I just won the Super Bowl!" Instead, he said, "Mom, happy birthday!" and he gave her a big hug. That was pretty cool.

There are a lot of demands on Thomas. When he goes places, people always want something from him. A picture. An autograph. A conversation. I still marvel at how engaging he is with fans and how he and his wife, Lauren, never seem frustrated.

He still greets people with the same grace and joy he did when he was a rookie.

For you young readers, I hope you learn this from my son's story: nice guys do win, but you have to persevere, and you can't lose sight of how important your education is. Thomas got into Southern Methodist University on an academic scholarship, and then he walked onto the football team.

The rest is history.

CHAPTER 1

FAMILY HISTORY

My mom's name is Isobel. She grew up on a farm in Bilsby, a small village in the district of Lincolnshire, England. Grandpa Don and his family survived World War II, with blackouts and food rations, so he was proud of his farm and his ability to build and provide for his own family.

My dad's name is John. He moved to England
after living in Argentina. Naturally, because of his
connection to those two countries, the constant of
my dad's childhood was soccer. When Dad was a boy,
the most popular team in England was Manchester
United. The club's games were usually televised. Dad's
favorite soccer memory as a kid was watching the
1970 World Cup.

England, the defending champion,
lost to West Germany 3-2

Dad's mother used to send him to get strawberries from a field. He would grab a basket, pick strawberries, weigh them, and pay per pound. That's where my dad met my mom, who was working there for the summer.

They both say it was love at first sight. When Dad moved to Minnesota, they wrote letters to each other all the time. Sometimes, Mom would edit some of Dad's letters and send them back.

Mom moved to the United States, and both she and Dad attended McNeese State University, a university in Louisiana that is close to the Texas border and 30 miles from the Gulf of Mexico. After they graduated, Dad got a job with Conoco, so they married and moved to Texas.

CHAPTER 2

THOMAS IS BORN

My dad almost didn't make it to the hospital when I was born. I was eager to enter the world. I arrived three weeks earlier than expected!

Like most mothers, my mom had some concerns about me. People did not tell her that I was a cute baby and my eyes were often crossed.

One day, shortly after I was born, my mom was talking on the phone to her mother.

"Mom, how do you know if you have an ugly baby?" she asked. "I don't know, Isobel. I had six babies, but I never had an ugly one," her mother responded.

I thought I was a pretty good-looking baby!

That pacifier was
one of my favorites!

CHAPTER 3

BAKER BOY

SURPRISE!

Mom realizes that I was making her a cake for Mother's Day...

CHAPTER 4

CHILDHOOD HOME

In June, when I was three, Dad was watching Wimbledon, the famous tennis tournament in England. Mom wanted to go look at a house not too far away that she thought would be better for the family.

Mom worked as an executive assistant at a large gas company, and Dad worked as a chemical engineer. The first home they bought in the Houston area was in a good neighborhood, but all the houses looked the same.

The house mom found was a brand new home on a cul-de-sac, which is a street closed at one end. It had a big yard and lots of towering pine trees.

Mom loved it. Dad did too. It was more than they had planned on spending, but they felt like it would be worth it.

Mom and Dad found a church they really liked that wasn't too far from the new house. During church, I would sometimes get antsy. Mom scribbled something on a piece of scrap paper.

If there are 10 cookies, how many do Sam and Rachel each get?

"Can you figure this out?" Mom asked. Thomas thought about it and then whispered back, "Five each." "Great, Thomas, you just did division!"

I discovered my passion for math in church. I really liked numbers.

CHAPTER 5

REPLACEMENT GLASSES

My left and right eye didn't work together, so one would "drift." Some people call that having a "lazy eye."

Wearing glasses was fine. Keeping them?

Not again. That's the fourth pair he's lost!

My eyes weren't the only thing I was insecure about.

You look like a chipmunk!

The person who made fun of me most lived in my neighborhood.

What's up chipmunk?

Chipmunk, chipmunk!

He didn't just say that once. Or twice...
He said it all the time. Finally, I told my Mom.

People are not always nice. But you must love yourself and put the problem on them.

Talking to Mom felt good. Even better, she helped me come up with a response to that mean kid.

Hey Chipmunk!

HA HA HA

I'm sorry you feel that way. But I'm fine with my teeth.

I'm glad your eyes work, and you can see well!

You look good on the outside and even better on the inside!

I appreciated how Mom and Dad supported me. They were always so positive.

I'm glad you're going to be on my team!

What position do you want to play?

Because I knew what it felt like to be picked on, I made sure to choose the kids who were made fun of for their size, looks, or lack of skill.

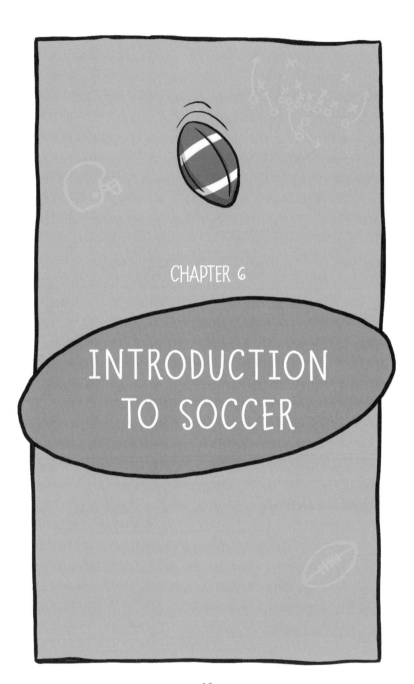

CHAPTER 6

INTRODUCTION
TO SOCCER

The first sport I tried, of course, was soccer. My parents signed me up for a nearby team called the South Belt Soccer Club. When I got to practice, I was very nervous about how well I would do on a team with lots of talented Hispanic players. Even the coach, George Dominguez, was Hispanic. James and I were the only two players who were not.

Coach Dominguez was kind and positive. He really liked soccer, and he always made it fun for us.

Coach Dominguez's Lesson:
Discipline comes first.
Soccer comes second.

Even Coach's son would sometimes act silly, and Coach disciplined him the same as the rest of us.

←COACH DOMINGUEZ

↖RANDY, THE COACH'S SON

Our team won some games, and we lost some games. I mostly played goalkeeper. Kicking the ball was my favorite part of playing goalie.

In one game, we were up 8-0, and Coach Dominguez
pulled me from the goal and played me at forward
with about 10 minutes to go. I was thrilled. When
James passed the ball to me, I excitedly dribbled
the ball up the field, zigzagging between and past
opponents. I fired a shot...and I missed.

A minute later, I stole the ball, dribbled past a defender, and shot the ball again. This time, the ball blew past the goalie. It was my first goal.

It was the most exhilarating feeling to watch the ball hit the back of the net!

CHAPTER 7

CRAB LESSON

When I was four years old, I was very excited because a bulldozer came to our house to dig a big hole.

This was something Mom always dreamed of us having, and part of why we moved into this house.

YUCK! That looks gross. I don't want to swim in green water!

Dad explained that the green color was from algae, which could be harmful. Using chemicals in the water kills the algae making the pool safe to swim in.

Mom wanted us to become good swimmers, so she signed us up for lessons at the YMCA.

Anytime someone was in the pool, Mom or Dad was watching. They were like the lifeguards!

I only had one problem when my parents signed me up for the Y's Swim Team

In swimming, there are four main types of strokes to move in the water.

FREESTYLE   That's the one that looks like you're crawling in the water, rolling your body from side to side and steadily turning to the side of the arm that is pulling water in. This was my best stroke.

BREASTSTROKE   This is often the first stroke taught to beginners because you can do it without goggles and with your head above water. To do it fast though, you dive under the water and explode out and forward. It was one of my worst strokes.

BUTTERFLY   This is an advanced stroke that people often struggle to learn. The dolphin kick has to be done with your legs moving up and down together. It's probably the most tiring stroke, but it was my second best.

BACKSTROKE   This is where you lie on your back and pull your body through the water with your arms. Your legs alternately flutter kick, and your head remains above the water. This was not one of my better strokes because I had a hard time staying in a straight line.

At one swimming meet, when I was nine, my coach needed me to swim the individual medley, which is all four strokes. I finished last, but I'll never forget my parents' reaction.

I was awful. That was so embarrassing.

What are you talking about? That was your first time, and you did your best! We're so proud of you.

LESSON FROM DAD
The crab only exits the shell to find a bigger shell. Putting yourself out there to be vulnerable is a sign of strength, not weakness. Great job.

CHAPTER 8

OVERSEAS ADVENTURE

Tomorrow is my first trip to visit family in England! I want to stay up all night so I can sleep on the boring 10-hour flight from Houston to London.

We were leaving Houston at night, so we enjoyed dinner at Pappadeaux.

It was my first international flight, and the pilot invited me into the cockpit after we reached cruising altitude!

How do you figure out what all of those buttons and levers do?

We have to learn and practice a lot.

It was a long drive from London to Grandad's farm in Northeast Lincolnshire, so we always stopped for a proper English Breakfast.

We had so many fun, new adventures.

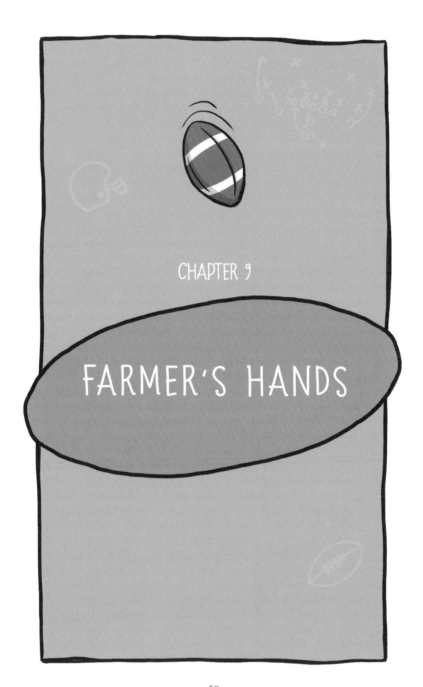

CHAPTER 9

FARMER'S HANDS

The family calls him Grandpa Don. I call him Grandad. His farm spans 2,000 acres, which is virtually the same as 2,000 football fields combined. He will never forget growing up during World War II and making nine dollars a week when he was first married. Those were challenging years.

We had to ration food, but we were grateful to have something to eat.

I always looked up to Grandad and cherished every minute with him. Those moments were sometimes hard to come by; he worked sunup to sundown. There were so many things he had to do every single day.

Grandad did not have a college education, but he was such a smart businessman, and he loved learning and trying new things. He was an award-winning photographer and had his own darkroom where he processed and printed his photos. I thought he was the coolest person ever!

Something that always amazed me about Grandad was his hands. They were calloused, meaning the skin was hardened from all his hard work. But his hands were essential tools on the farm, operating important machines, handling animals, and harvesting vegetables.

I learned so much from Grandad because he was very wise. One of the most incredible projects I ever saw him work on was an old caravan he found in a field. It was in terrible shape. Over the course of a few years he rebuilt the caravan, making it something truly magical.

Grandad's Rule:

Things don't happen overnight. Lay a good foundation when you are young, so you have a good direction for life. Hang your hat on working hard and having a good attitude.

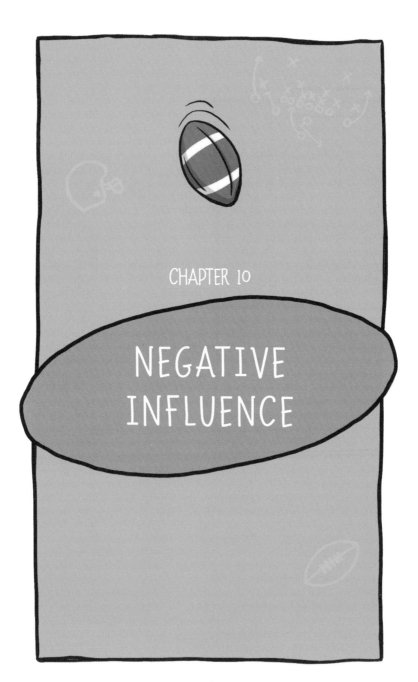

CHAPTER 10

NEGATIVE
INFLUENCE

My family loved our neighborhood, especially living in a cul-de-sac. My mom really liked it because fewer cars traveled onto our street. My brother Patrick and I played with some of the neighbors, especially one named Tyler. He was two years younger than me, but he was taller, stronger, and faster. One of our favorite activities was playing roller hockey with two nets. We played hockey for hours. The first person to score 100 points was declared the winner.

We competed in everything: baseball, basketball, football, and hockey. We usually got along, but sometimes we would get into arguments.

Sometimes one of us would storm away
and need some time to cool off.

The boy who called me Chipmunk moved away. But there was another neighbor who often made me feel uncomfortable. His name was Peter, and he always invited me over to his house to hang out. One day, when it was raining outside, I was bored and decided to go.

I wasn't even allowed to watch a PG-13 movie, advised for children 13 or older. Rated R? Definitely not! I abruptly told Peter I had to go home. He called me a scaredy-cat, but I didn't care.

I was panting as I told my mom what happened.

"Am I in trouble?" I asked her once she knew the story. "No, Thomas, you were smart to trust your instincts. You know what's right and what's wrong."

CHAPTER 11

POWER OF WORDS

Patrick and I didn't like to get up early on the weekends, especially on Sundays. But Mom would wake us up and treat us to Shipley's for kolaches on our way to church. Kolaches are pastries with sausage, egg, or cheese in them. Patrick and I loved sausage kolaches, which are sometimes called pigs in a blanket.

Church was about six miles from home, and Mom rotated as a Sunday School teacher with two other women. On the days she taught, we'd have to leave home earlier than usual, but she loved volunteering at church and keeping us connected to other church families. One of my favorite church friends was Jen, who I played many games of Tic-tac-toe against over the years.

Mom liked to share Bible lessons, but she said one thing more than anything else.

Mom's rule:

Always share, care, and encourage.

When I was 10 years old, I didn't live that message out. Mom was running late to pick me up at home and take me to a soccer game that was scheduled to start at 6 p.m. I didn't just like to be on time; I always wanted to be early. I unloaded on her in the car.

A lump started to develop in my throat just as the words spilled out of my mouth. I had never felt worse. Mom pulled over on the side of the road. We didn't say anything for a few minutes. After I calmed down, I apologized. We drove to the game, and I was 15 minutes late.

My heart wasn't in that game.

I didn't play well, and I don't even remember if we won or lost.

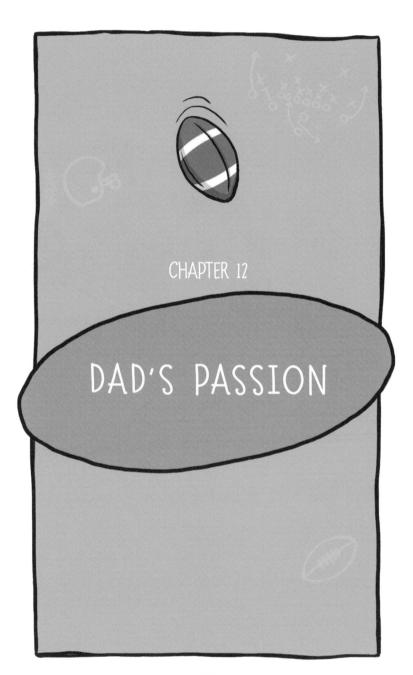

CHAPTER 12

DAD'S PASSION

Dad helped provide for our family by working as a chemical engineer. He also trained as a cyclist. Three days a week he would go on 12-mile bike rides, completing three, four-mile loops around our neighborhood. On Saturdays and Sundays, he would ride 80 to 130 miles!

I watched from the side of the road as cyclists breezed by. I thought my dad looked pretty cool. He was often toward the front of the pack. I remember the first time I stood in the Feed Zone. It was during the Texas Road Racing State Championship. That race is 100 miles with eight loops of 12 ½ miles each. I got to help in the Feed Zone that time because one of the regular workers wasn't there.

I was nervous. I didn't know what to expect. I asked an older person what I should do and where I should go. He was very patient with me. He explained that the cyclists would come past at about 30 miles per hour and grab what they needed: a water bottle, protein bar, fruit, or beef jerky.

Tour de France cyclists burn over 6,000 calories a day. That's the same as eating 20 slices of pizza or nine burgers.

Dad was a great sprinter, and he moved up several spots to finish third.

I couldn't believe it. Dad's friend said it was customary for a rider to give his helper five percent of his winnings, but it wasn't about the money for me. I had fun, and I got to help my dad.

On the drive home, with the bike on the back of the car, I listened intently to my dad.

Dad's Rule:
Have the discipline to pursue something with passion.

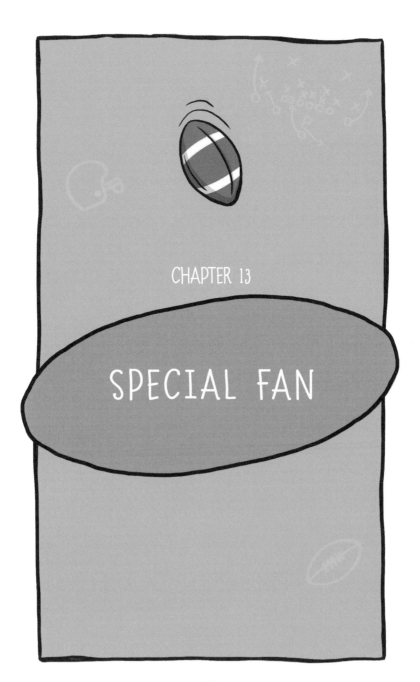

CHAPTER 13

SPECIAL FAN

I hardly paid attention to who was on the sidelines of our games. But I was really, really excited when my cousin Daniel asked to come to one of my games. I was 11, and he was seven years younger than me. I felt nervous playing in front of him.

I felt something funny in my stomach with Daniel watching.

In that game, I missed my first shot, sending the ball way over the crossbar. A few minutes later, I received the ball outside the penalty box, dribbled hard toward the middle, and drilled the ball into the bottom right corner of the goal. I felt relieved. And that was just the beginning.

Wow, Thomas got a hat trick!

It was so great to have Daniel watch me play that day. I sort of assumed everyone's parents attended every game because mine never missed one. Then I realized how wrong I was. Midway through the season, my teammate Carlos was super excited at practice.

Carlos told us that his mom and dad weren't together, and that his dad lived in El Paso. That's also in Texas but nearly 11 hours away! Texas is a big state. Carlos wanted to score a goal in front of his dad, and I wanted to help him.

We won the game 3-0, but Carlos missed both of his shot attempts. I made mine, but I wished Carlos had scored instead.

On the drive home, I didn't mention Carlos to my
parents, but I thanked them for coming. I realized
that I took for granted how hard they worked to be
at all of my games and other events.

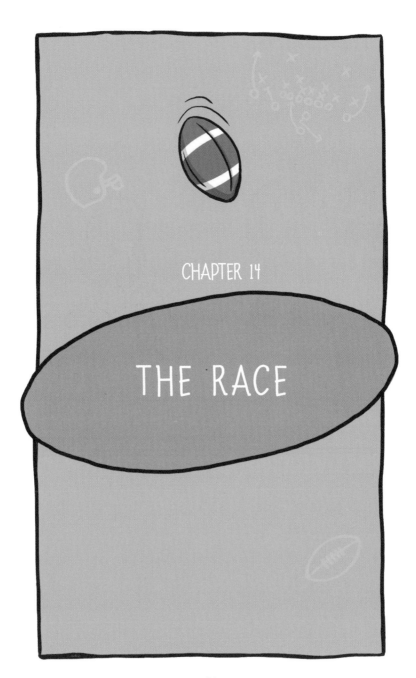

CHAPTER 14

THE RACE

The tradition of schools in our district was to have races on the first day. At Shadycrest Elementary School, we raced each other during recess, and I almost always finished first or second. I was thrilled to win the 200- and 800-meter races. It meant I would get to advance to the district finals, which included five other elementary schools.

There were at least 200 people watching the district finals, and there was a long wait for the races to begin. For the second time in my life, I felt butterflies in my stomach. Then another kid started to trash talk me, and I wasn't nervous anymore.

I'm going to win, and I'm going to destroy you!

I didn't even respond. Instead, I ignored him.

When the 200-meter race started, I fell behind and was in last place after 20 meters. But I wasn't worried; I was never a strong starter. Halfway through the race, I passed one opponent. Sometimes I got tired at this point in a race, but I felt a surge of energy on this day. My dad later told me that was called adrenaline. I took the lead with 50 meters to go.

As an athlete, that was my proudest moment. I took my place atop the podium. I'll never forget the rush of receiving the big blue ribbon. My parents and Patrick were cheering from the stands. It looked like they were very proud of me. I was proud of myself too.

CHAPTER 15

COACH SHOWS
CHARACTER

I loved what the world calls football (soccer), but I also loved what Americans call football. In seventh grade, at Pearland Junior High West, I wanted to play on the football team, but it was very intimidating. Over 100 kids showed up to try out for the team, and a lot of them were clearly more qualified than I was.

I made the B team initially. Later, tryouts for kickers and punters took place, and I excelled. Then the A team coach tried to convince me to play for him. But Coach Craft, the B team coach, was very encouraging and said it was my choice. Coach Craft told me kicking and punting would be heavily emphasized on the B team, and I would also get to play other positions.

I chose to play on the B team.

We had a pretty good season, and I also got to play receiver and return some punts. I even scored three touchdowns! But our finale was against our rival: Pearland Junior High East. The game was so big Coach

Craft gave us his first real pep talk of the season. The game was tense, and there was no score heading into the fourth quarter. On third down, with three seconds left, our offense got to the two-yard line, and I prepared to attempt a 19-yard field goal.

I disagreed with Coach Craft, but I was too respectful to question him out loud. I headed back to the sideline. On fourth down, our running back took the handoff and sprinted through a hole, but two defenders smashed him and he stopped a yard short of the end zone.

Game over. Scoreless tie.

Coach Craft had another surprise for me.

I was stunned. I felt like Coach Craft really cared about me. I wasn't disappointed for long. We tied that game, but we won several others and, most importantly, I had a blast!

CHAPTER 16

BOXING DAY PARTY

We loved spending Christmas in England. My Grandad had a game called, "Dip In The Bag." Each kid got one shot to stick both hands and grab as many English coins as possible!

Bilsby

I hope I got a bunch of dollar coins!

We brought the tradition back to Pearland.

England, Wales, Scotland, and Northern Ireland comprise the United Kingdom. The day after Christmas, the UK celebrates Boxing Day, which may date back to the Middle Ages. The tradition was for employers to give employees a small box that contained money, food, clothes, and other valuables.

Boxing Day is still an official public holiday in many countries. Stores have big sales, and lots of professional soccer games are played.

MORSTEAD FAMILY
BOXING DAY PARTY
DECEMBER 26TH
6-9 PM
DINNER, DESSERT & DRINKS SERVED

In Pearland, we invited friends, neighbors and church members to celebrate Boxing Day at our house. Sometimes there were upwards of 20 people!

The history of Boxing Day goes back a long, long time...

We played lots of games, including Trivial Pursuit and charades.

The highlight for our guests was the White Elephant Gift Exchange. Everyone brought a gift...but there were rules.

Gifts had to be wrapped and worth less than $10. Everyone piled the gifts in the center and randomly drew numbers. The first person opened a gift. The second person could "steal" that gift or open an unwrapped one. The game continued until everyone had a gift.

The game got pretty wild!

What is this?

That's a garden gnome.

Just like in England, the best part of our Boxing Day celebration was enjoying time with family and friends.

CHAPTER 17

SHOPPING
WITH JEN

I pretty much wore the same clothes in elementary and most of middle school: a T-shirt or jersey with shorts or sweatpants, and sneakers. I started to notice girls and boys at school wearing much nicer clothes, so I decided to upgrade my wardrobe, but I had no idea who to ask for help! Definitely not my dad or brother. Or my mom. Finally, I came up with the perfect person.

Jen was fashionable and everyone thought she was cool.

Jen and I had known each other through church since we were in preschool, and our families—who lived just five minutes apart—often hung out. We even played percussion in the band together.

Time was running out before the start of eighth grade, and we still hadn't gone shopping. Jen came over to hang out, and Mom overheard her asking me about getting new clothes.

My mom smiled. She handed me $200 to buy clothes and offered to drop us off at Baybrook Mall. I was kind of nervous.

Jen had strong opinions on what I should wear, and she handed me stuff to try on. I didn't protest. We walked all over the mall, and Jen helped me pick out a bunch of clothes. After two hours, we were hungry. I had enough money left to buy us chicken sandwiches and fries.

When my mom came to pick us up, I had four bags of new clothes. I felt pretty good about how I would look when I went back to school.

CHAPTER 18

BEST GIFT EVER

Make sure you follow through.

On a trip to England, my Uncle Charlie taught me how to play rugby.

I couldn't believe it, but I picked up rugby so quickly that my cousin's team invited me to practice and scrimmage with them.

CHAPTER 19

BE COMFORTABLE BEING UNCOMFORTABLE

Our church was like a family. If someone got sick, others rallied around them by providing meals and starting prayer chains. We were definitely not a mega-church, but we had hundreds of members who regularly attended not only on Sundays but also for events and meetings throughout the week. I remember Dad helping a new family at church pay an expensive car repair bill.

Patrick and I were a part of the youth group, though Mom and Dad didn't really give us a choice. A lot of the kids were our friends anyway.

One of the activities that always made me feel uneasy was going door-to-door telling people about our church and, if there were kids at the home, inviting them to youth group.

Converting or seeking to convert someone to Christianity was a core part of our church's beliefs. That's called evangelism, and our pastor expected us to go into all types of neighborhoods and tell them about our church and faith. Mr. Habermast supervised us, and he asked why I wasn't acting like my usual self.

I'm afraid I won't have the right answers to people's questions.

LESSON FROM MR. HABERMAST
In order to grow, you must learn to be comfortable being uncomfortable.

Mr. Habermast added that no one, including himself,

had all the right answers or knew all the Scriptures.

That made me feel a lot better. When people we had

invited to church actually came, I'm not sure there

was a more satisfying feeling!

CHAPTER 20

DAD'S WRECK

I was always amazed by how well my dad did in racing. I had heard most of the riders were professionals or only worked part-time jobs. My dad worked as a chemical engineer by day, and he trained vigorously in the evenings and on weekends. He transformed our garage into his own gym, and he never missed a workout.

In middle and high school, I had been to many races. I always liked being on Dad's team. I usually handed him the Musette, a small bag we put food or a drink bottle in that he could snatch as he whipped by the Feed Zone. Even without looking at a watch, I could sense when my dad was going to come by. But at a big championship one time, I watched the lead pack blow by...and I didn't see him.

A few minutes later a van pulled up, and I saw Dad inside. He didn't have his helmet on, and he was holding a white towel in his right hand over his left ear. I was really worried.

My dad had suffered injuries before. He had broken a collarbone and once had "road rash" and nearly lost half the skin on his legs after a fall. But cycling was something he had loved since he was my age, and he was one of the best around. We headed to the hospital to get him fixed up.

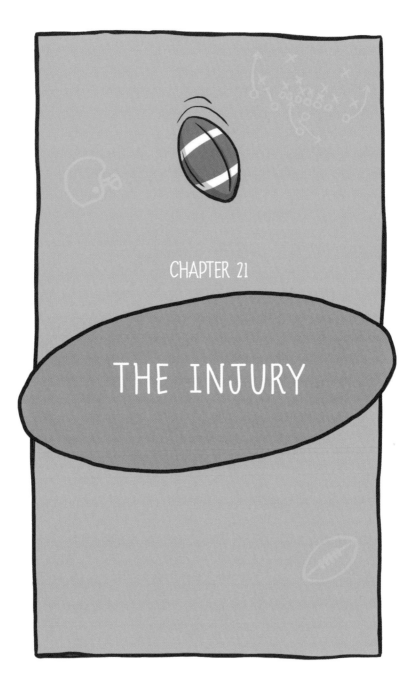

CHAPTER 21

THE INJURY

Remember how 100 kids tried out for the middle school football team? Well, twice that many came out for the high school freshman team! In Texas, football is the most popular sport, no matter what level: NFL all the way down to Pee Wee.

At the time, the Dallas Cowboys could be considered the NFL's most popular team, and their games were not to be missed on Sundays. Millions of people in Texas also watch football on Saturdays when college teams play and on Fridays when high school teams compete. A lot of movies and television shows have been based on football in Texas.

I was one of the smaller players, but I was still the best kicker. I could boot the ball way further than anyone on my team and most of the kickers on opposing teams. The coaches recognized that, and I made the team.

In a scrimmage against Westside High, I spent too much time admiring my first kickoff sailing through the air.

I felt excruciating pain in my left leg as the trainer carefully checked on me. My mom had to drive onto the field to get me. I couldn't stop crying. On the ride to the hospital, I could feel every bump on the road. Once I was in the emergency room, I had to wait two hours to get an x-ray.

I had suffered a broken tibia and fibula in my left leg. The doctor had to set my leg in a cast and explained that it would be months before I regained the full use of my leg. That meant I would miss the rest of the football season. I was really sad, but my Grandad cheered me up and encouraged me to grow from this injury.

When I was healthy again, I was relieved that I could run like I had before. In soccer, I was still scoring lots of goals for my club team. In the fall, I made the football team again, but I kept getting drilled in practices. So, I decided I didn't want to play football anymore. The funny thing is, that's when I really started to grow.

CHAPTER 22

OFFICIAL JOB

When I was 14, I started training sessions to become a soccer official. I even had to pass a test.

I took pride in my job.

THROW-IN

SUBSTITUTION

OFFSIDE

OFFSIDE

I was always a little anxious about dealing with an angry coach or parent. I didn't like confrontation.

Fortunately, that coach backed down and mumbled an apology.

125

The following fall, I attended the soccer tryouts, but I was shocked to discover that I not only didn't make the varsity team, I didn't even make the JV team!

Is there anything I can improve on to make the team next season?

Don't bother coming back. You will not make the team.

I am so sorry you have to deal with this.

How can he do this? This is the worst day of my life.

LESSON FROM DAD
Life isn't always fair.

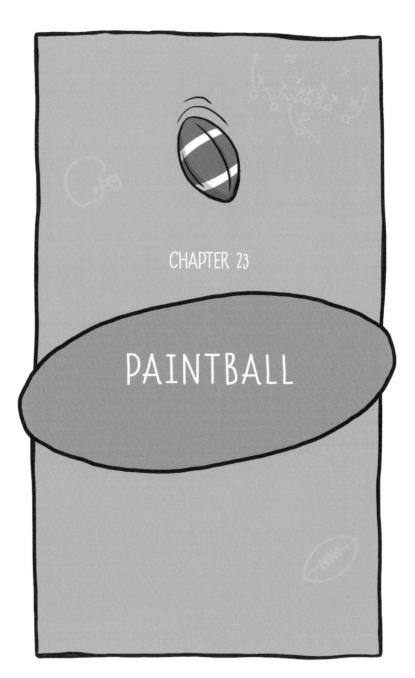

CHAPTER 23

PAINTBALL

My brother Patrick and I got along well enough, but we really didn't have much in common. I obviously loved sports, and he really didn't. Even worse for him, I was almost always the last player off the field. Since he couldn't stay home alone, Mom or Dad usually brought him along to pick me up.

Patrick's favorite activity was paintball, a high-energy activity in which players wield air weapons that fire dye-filled gelatin capsules. Players wear protective gear and compete either individually or in teams in a variety of scenarios. Patrick would go to paintball games as often as our parents allowed, which was usually at least once a week.

I wasn't into paintball, but our youth group went when I was a sophomore. I'm not sure I've ever seen Patrick more excited! He suggested I wear a long-sleeve shirt and pants because the paintballs sting if

Patrick competed in local tournaments

you get hit. Patrick even let me borrow one of his

air weapons, but I had no idea what I was getting

myself into.

I was clueless when it came to paintball. As I was looking in one direction, Patrick came up behind me, readying his weapon to shoot. Just as I spun around, he nailed me.

Patrick dominated everyone! I couldn't ever figure out where he was, and he seemed to hit me more than anyone else.

CHAPTER 24

PSYCHED OUT
BY PHYSICS

I wasn't where I wanted to be as an athlete, but I was definitely where I wanted to be as a student. I challenged myself with one of the most demanding schedules at my school.

Advanced Placement is college-level curriculum for high school students. You can complete classes and even take exams that can earn you college credits.

One of my favorite teachers was Mrs. Tate. She made Chemistry fun, and she was always so positive. I was lucky to have her for two years. She seemed like she really loved her job.

I was intimidated heading into my senior year. I had already signed up for AP classes in English, Calculus, Government, and Economics. Could I really handle AP Physics too?

Mrs. Tate didn't teach AP Physics, but I wanted to get her advice.

Then Mrs. Tate provided a perspective that I really needed to hear. She said people often underestimate themselves, and she insisted I not make that mistake.

Mrs. Tate's Rule:
Don't doubt yourself.
You can do more than
you think.

Mrs. Tate was right. I worked really hard my senior year, and it all paid off.

CHAPTER 25

DEFINING MOMENT

The football team had won two games in four seasons before Coach Heath arrived. He wanted me to help build up the Oilers program.

I wasn't one of the smallest kids anymore. I outgrew clothes and shoes really quickly in high school.

I may have been 6 foot 3, but my role on the team was to kick the football.

We had an incredible season. Our second-round playoff game was at the Astrodome, the longtime home of the Houston Astros and Oilers!

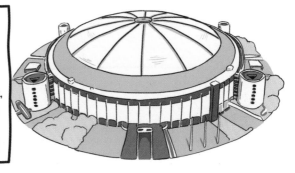

In that game, we faced one of the top football players in the state, Jamaal Charles of Memorial High School in Port Arthur. He was a dynamic running back who would eventually star at the University of Texas and then in the National Football League.

Jamaal scored four touchdowns! But our team battled and put me in a position to kick a game-tying extra point with two minutes remaining. I followed my routine, taking a deep breath just before the snap and kick.

I struck the ball well, but it drifted and drilled the left upright.

BONK

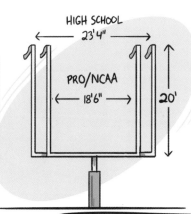

HIGH SCHOOL
23'4"

PRO/NCAA
18'6"

20'

I knew the high school goalpost was wider than the pro goalpost. But I refused to make any excuses.

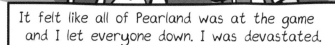

That's not fair. That would have been good on a high school goalpost!

No excuses. That was all my responsibility.

It felt like all of Pearland was at the game and I let everyone down. I was devastated.

I'm really proud of Thomas for not blaming anyone or anything else.

I was still hurting, but hearing my Dad say that about me made me feel much better.

CHAPTER 26

HELPING JAMES

James and I had known each other since we were six years old. We had a lot in common, namely being soccer players and kickers.

We spent a lot of time hanging out and practicing our kicks.

We went to different high schools and James ended up becoming the varsity kicker in his sophomore year. He stopped hanging out with me. His football team was doing well, and he was spending all of his time with teammates. He started to go to parties.

James and I still talked once in a while. He wanted to reconnect when we were seniors. He felt like he was being a hypocrite, attending Fellowship of Christian Athletes meetings on Wednesdays and then partying on Fridays.

I was thrilled to spend time with James again.
He came over often, and we worked out in my
dad's garage gym.

On weekends, we would lift and run, and hang out
and watch movies. Our favorite movie was Rocky.
We would be so fired up after the movie that we
would go work out again.

James and I had really good senior years. I think our friendship helped us both that way.

CHAPTER 27

MAKING PLANS

I always looked up to my Uncle Stuart. He was so smart. He worked at a management consulting company that helped businesses, nonprofits, and even government agencies.

Early in my senior year, Uncle Stuart offered to pay me to help him with a home project. First, we headed to a home improvement store to get supplies. Uncle Stuart pulled out a big binder with different supplies and phases of his renovation projects.

I was blown away by Uncle Stuart's plans. We didn't

say much on the seven-minute ride back to his house.

Colleges were recruiting me for academics, but deep down, I wanted to be a collegiate athlete.

I didn't know anything about the process; fortunately, Uncle Stuart did a ton of research. He helped me put together a highlight tape and track down addresses for a bunch of coaches.

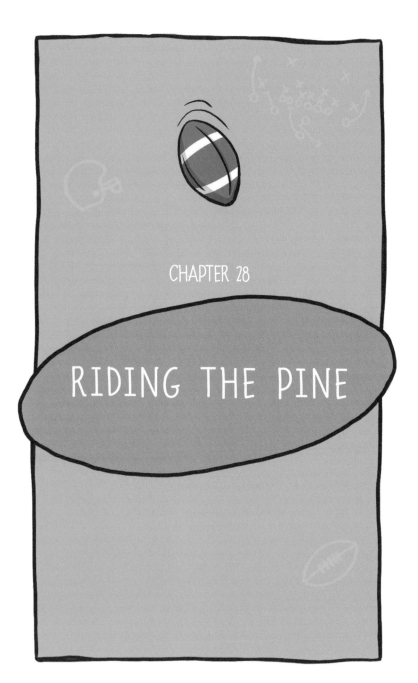

CHAPTER 28

RIDING THE PINE

Coach Hanson was still the varsity soccer coach during my senior season. I remembered what he told me, but I decided to go to tryouts anyway. I figured I had nothing to lose.

I felt so confident at the tryout and scored several goals.

Coach Hanson said he'd post the names on the varsity roster on Thursday morning. He wasn't mean to me during the three-day tryout. As soon as the roster was up, we crowded around to see who made the team. My eyes scanned the page, looking intently for my name. When I saw that it was on the list, I was ecstatic! I made the team!

Coach Hanson immediately pulled me aside to have a chat.

That felt so unfair, but it wasn't a shock; Coach Hanson had said I would never play for him. Instead of feeling sorry for myself, I pondered the bigger question: did I love soccer enough that I would practice but not play?

I decided to join the team anyway. To get more of my soccer fix, I played with an indoor team. My dad also believed I deserved to play on the school soccer team, but he told me he was proud of how I handled it all.

Dad's Rule:
Things will not always
go your way.
Don't let someone else
dictate your joy.

EPILOGUE

Thomas Morstead was not recruited as an athlete by colleges while at Pearland High School in the spring of 2004. The reason he could accept admission into Southern Methodist University (SMU) was because he earned a partial engineering scholarship. He immediately walked onto the football team but had to wait to play.

He redshirted his first season and did not make an appearance until taking over place-kicking and punting duties as a redshirt sophomore in 2006. He led Conference USA by averaging 43.8 yards per punt.

He also made 13 of 18 field goals and 34 of 35 extra points.

His best season was in 2007, when he was a first-team All-Conference USA pick by both the coaches and the media. He led the conference and ranked ninth in the nation with a 44.6-yard average. Of 57 punts, he landed 21 inside the 20 and only four were touchbacks. His season long was a 72-yarder. He also made all 43 extra points and 13-of-20 field goals, including three over 50 yards.

Thomas developed into one of the top punters in the nation, a distinction he largely credits to Jamie Kohl.

Starting in 2004, Thomas started attending Kohl's kicking camps.

"He's the premier kicking coach in the world," Thomas told SB Nation in 2019. "He is my oldest son's godfather, and my best friend. We went on this journey together."

The New Orleans Saints moved up in the 2009 NFL Draft and selected Thomas in the fifth round with the 164th overall pick. He beat out veteran Glenn Pakulak and played in all 16 games. But he shined in the postseason with an NFL-best 44.8 net on 13 punts and six touchbacks on kickoffs. In Super Bowl XLIV, Thomas keyed the execution of one of the greatest special teams plays ever. Down 10-6 to the Indianapolis Colts at halftime, Saints coach Sean Payton told his players in the locker room that they would try an onside kick to start the third quarter.

Negative thoughts overwhelmed him during halftime, but Thomas remembered a message from one of the most influential people in his life. Frank Gansz Sr. coached Thomas during his senior year at SMU and impacted him in profound ways. Gansz died the day after the Saints drafted Thomas. One Gansz insight that Thomas reflected on was that the more aggressive team usually won. That lifted the anxiety from Thomas. When the moment arrived, Thomas booted a near-perfect onside kick, and Saints teammate Chris Reis recovered the ball.

"When I saw it all happen, I was obviously upset because that isn't a fantastic way to start a half, especially in the Super Bowl," Colts punter Pat McAfee told ESPN.com. "But now that I've had a chance to really dissect it and watch it numerous times, it's one of the most impressive kicks ever. Thomas Morstead will go down as one of the most accomplished punters to ever walk this earth."

The Saints scored a touchdown on the ensuing series and dominated the second half en route to a 31-17 victory.

Thomas and quarterback Drew Brees are the only two players from that championship team who remain on the Saints roster. Thomas was selected for the Pro Bowl and All-Pro teams in 2012, and he was named Pro Football Focus Special Teams Player of the Year in 2018.

Widely considered one of the NFL's best punters, Thomas signed a five-year extension with the Saints during the 2018 offseason.

In 2013, Thomas married his longtime girlfriend Lauren in their hometown of Houston. The following year they founded What You Give Will Grow, as a way to help the New Orleans community—especially children battling cancer—and encourage the giving spirit. The foundation name was inspired by Gansz.

"My favorite quote of his is 'What you give will grow, and what you keep you lose.' That always resonated with me," Thomas says. "I knew I wanted to honor him in some way once I made it into the NFL."

In January 2018, the Saints were on the verge of pulling off a dramatic comeback against the Minnesota Vikings. They overcame a 17-0 deficit and took a 24-23 lead with 25 seconds remaining. But on the final play of the game, Vikings quarterback Case Keenum connected with receiver Stefon Diggs on what would be a 61-yard touchdown pass. Many Saints left the field, but NFL rules did not allow for the game to officially end until the Vikings' point-after attempt.

Thomas was the first Saints player to return to the field, a classy act recognized by Viking fans who honored him by making donations to What You Give Will Grow. Thomas returned to Minnesota just before Super Bowl LII and handed a $221,000 check to Minnesota's Children's Hospital.

Thomas and Lauren have made their home in New Orleans, where each of their four children (Maxwell, Beckett, Maggie, and Rosalie) were born.

"In spite of his great success, there's nothing arrogant about him," says Pastor Charles Learman, who baptized Thomas as a baby. "He is very kind and gracious to people, and that has gone a long, long way."

THOMAS'S LIFE RULE:

In the process of putting this book together, I've realized one of my greatest strengths is never settling. I've always been willing to work hard, and I persevered through some early disappointments and struggles. Later, I discovered those obstacles were blessings. I wouldn't be the man I am today, had I not experienced them. In everything I do, I push myself to not settle for the easiest path but to strive for the best one.

ACKNOWLEDGMENTS

FROM THOMAS MORSTEAD

I must start by thanking God, who has granted me this opportunity to share my story to bless others.

I'd like to thank my parents for all their sacrifices and the love and stability I was provided as a child. My brother Patrick was the best man at my wedding, and he aptly said of our parents, "We are thankful for the model that you provided us by not telling us but showing us how to live."

I'd like to thank all the people who made this book possible: Lindsey Mitchell, Dennis Lomonaco, Sean Jensen, and the team at BroadStreet Publishing.

I also want to thank Lauren for being the glue of our family. The life we are building is better than I ever thought possible. I am so excited for our future together.

To Maxwell, Beckett, Maggie and Rosalie: I look forward to reading this book to you. Hopefully, some of my experiences will help you as you grow up.

FROM SEAN JENSEN

I thank God for his love, grace, and mercy in my life.

I thank my wife Erica, who has steadily encouraged and inspired me since we started our relationship 25 years ago.

Thank you Lindsey Mitchell for initially connecting me, Dennis Lomonaco for your boundless energy and ideas, and Thomas Morstead and family for sharing your stories.

Thanks to illustrator Daniel Hawkins for seamlessly joining and blessing our Middle School Rules team.

Lastly, thank you to my children, Zarah and Elijah, for challenging and inspiring me every single day!

SEAN JENSEN was born in South Korea. He was adopted and grew up in California, Massachusetts, and Virginia, mostly on or near military bases. Given his unique background, Sean has always been drawn to storytelling, a skill he developed at Northwestern University and crafted as a sportswriter—almost exclusively covering the NFL. During his career, he's fostered strong relationships throughout pro sports. He is an inspirational speaker who hosts a weekly podcast called "Winning Is not Everything." The podcast aims to bring sanity back to youth sports through conversations with high-character athletes, coaches, and parents. He lives in Minneapolis with his wife, two kids, and a dog.